Heart Sijo

Alaska Inspired Photos and Poems

Dwayne Cole

Parson's Porch Books

Heart Sijo: Alaska Inspired Photos and Poems
ISBN: Softcover
Copyright © 2023 by Dwayne Cole

Parson's Porch Books is an imprint of Parson's Porch *&* Company (PP*&*C) in Cleveland, Tennessee. PP*&*C is a self-funded charity which earns money by publishing books of noted authors, representing all genres. Its face and voice is **David Russell Tullock** (dtullock@parsonsporch.com).

Parson's Porch *&* Company *turns books into bread & milk* by sharing its profits with the poor.

www.parsonsporch.com

Heart Sijo

I knew the first day I saw you,
   an adventure was under way.

Two flowers blossoming,
   in a duet of love.

Dancing in warm sunshine.
   Heart to heart for eternity.

I took the photo on the cover in May 2015, while walking with Beth. Beth and I met in seminary in 1964, and united our hearts as one in marriage in 1965. Standing in awe, we saw the flowers as a symbol of our love. As we clasped our hands, a deep feeling of love swept over us. The wish to live and experience this beauty and wonder is visible in all living things. In witnessing this heart language beauty, we were enlivened. I wrote these sijo poems to capture this adventurous enlightenment.

Forest bathing nature poems
   can heal old wounds.

Make us healthier,
   more creative, and happier.

Heart Sijo-- Poetry
   singing our soul awake.

Dedication

This book is dedicated to Chuck Newell and all educators who teach poetry. Chuck is an award-winning poet and educator who teaches as the English department chair at Notre Dame High School in Chattanooga, Tennessee. He is a contributing writer in the book, SIJO: Korea's Poetry Form, edited by Lucy Park and Elizabeth Jorgensen. Chuck graciously read my manuscript and encouraged me to seek publication. I had the privilege of serving as his pastor when I was senior minister of First Cumberland Presbyterian Church in Chattanooga. Poetry moves our world a little closer to beauty and wonder. I hope all who read my Heart Sijo poems will have this experience—

Sijo Mindfulness

All things are inter-related,
 and connected as one.

Open-hearted awareness,
 openness to each moment.

Cultivating enlightenment,
 kindness toward all entities.

Our Hearts Leaped

We saw this awesome sight
    of two hearts becoming one.

Memories trickle down cheeks,
    memories of marital love.

In the fields spring lilies blossom,
    opening star studded hands.

Introduction

Beth, and I enjoy poetry and wanted to share verses
with our grandchildren, as a way to nurture openness
with the beauty and wonder of nature. The three simple lines
of the small haiku, have traditionally been seen
as a good place to start teaching children a love of poetry.
Haiku uses inspiring nature scenes that enrich the lives
of teacher and student. Our grandchildren's art work and
poems helped us rediscover a child's wonder
in our lives. Seeing the sparkle in their eyes helped us
to see with the eyes of a child. The tears of joy washed
away some of life's travel stains that cloud our vision.

The wonder of a child blossomed anew in us,
becoming fertile ground for tender teachings.
After haiku, sijo is a logical next step in teaching poetry.
Sijo is a Korean style of lyrical poetry originally called "short
song." Sijo resembles Japanese haiku in having a foundation
in nature, but neither sijo nor haiku are limited to nature as
subject. Haiku is a short poem with three lines. The first and
third lines have 5 syllables each, the second line has 7
syllables. The syllable count may vary slightly. The emphasis
is on an economy of words.

Sijo has three lines with 14-16 syllables in each line, for a total
of 44-46 syllables. The count may vary slightly as in haiku. In
sijo, there is a pause in the middle of each line, so in English
they are sometimes printed in six lines instead of three. A
famous example of a sijo is this poem by Yun Seondo:

You ask how many friends I have?
 Water and stone, bamboo and pine.

The moon rising over the hill is a joyful comrade.

Besides these five companions, what other pleasure should I
ask?

Using this famous sijo as inspiration, I wrote the two below. The book, *Sijo: Korea's Poetry Form*, and my friend, Chuck Newell, one of its contributors, also inspired me to write this book.

My Alaska Friends

I have many Alaska friends—
    mountains, glaciers, waterfalls.

Moose, bears, eagles, and swans—
    All re-wilding my life with wonder.

Born from the wild things of nature—
    Nurtured as one in heart and soul.

Safe in Ark

In the old farm beaver pond,
    the guard slaps a warning sign.

The young dive into hut safely,
    snug and secure from all harm.

Evolution's ark formation—
    Home is a safe place to be.

Why Should One Read and Write Sijo?

In my retirement in Alaska for the last decade, I have become a contemplative, wedded to the natural beauty and wonder of what I see everyday. What I see in Alpenglow sunrises and sunsets shapes my poetry. This way of seeing is reflected in the subtitle, Alaska Inspired Photos and Poems. The title of my book, *Heart Sijo*, marks it as Korea's poetry form.

When you read my sijo, shaped by Korea's form of poetry, you'll come across Korean cultural ideas and idioms. Every language has idioms that come in all shapes and sizes. Korean culture is influenced by Confucian values—respect for family, elders, and authority.

Learning Korean sijo is a wonderful experience. You get a window into the history and wisdom of the language. In our culturally diverse world this can be a healthy healing experience.

An Asian proverb states: "It is better to see something once than to hear about it a thousand times." My hope for you is that these sijo poems will enable you to see life more clearly.

Some Guidelines for Teaching Sijo

In teaching poetry to our grandchildren, we read poetry to them. Then as they thought of writing their own poems, we asked these questions to stimulate their poetic thoughts.

1. What is your poem going to be about? Choose a subject.

2. What nature image can you use to portray your subject?

3. Introduce the subject you have chosen in the first line of your sijo with the syllable count 3-4-4-4.

4. Develop the theme or subject you have chosen in the second line with the syllable count 3-4-4-4.

5. Bring the subject to a close with a twist in the third line of your sijo with the syllable count 3-5, 4-3. The goal is to bring the subject to a close with a feeling of excitement. As in haiku this is often an aha moment. You might want to read the sijo in this book in light of these guidelines.

Heart Sijo

Hear a hermit thrush singing—
    A complete pentatonic scale.

With all harmonic intervals,
    sometimes moving up an octave!

Garden full of thrilling tones—
    Wish to be a hermit thrush.

Enlivenment

Nature comes alive in me,
    when I write sijo poetry.
Forest bathing enlivens,
    makes one more healthy and wise.

Joy comes in knowing we are one,
    with all other living things.

Purity of Snow

Trees and mountains covered in snow,
    blending together as one.

Snow owl lights on a tree branch,
    clutching a field mouse in claws.

Owlets tucked securely
    in Mother Nature's blanket.

Wrapped in Love

In Alaska's winter blizzards,
   snow falls incessantly.

Mountains, trees, skies become one—
   Wrapped in purity blanket.

I pull up my warm blanket,
   wrapped in tenderness and love.

Watched the moose, eyes kissing the snow,
lips nibbling frozen twigs breakfast.

Blizzard dreams rip the seams
of her green-growth dreams.

Sun shines through the leafless limbs.
Can spring be far behind?

(Photo taken from my deck in Anchorage)

Adventurous Ideas

Floating on billowing clouds,
    I had my first dream of the day.

Alpenglow mountains beaming,
    golden leaves humming the tune.

I beamed with joy and excitement,
    told no one my secret.

Come, let us watch the sunrise,
    and walk in the dawning light.

Remembering half-forgotten joys,
    become fully ripened fruit.

Committed to grow more tender—
    Nurtured in heaven's light.

Letting Go

Fall is making its exit—
  Winter is almost here.

Golden leaves are dancing,
  marching like toy soldiers.

Falling leaves teach us lessons—
  How to let loved ones go unafraid.

D. Cole

Wake-Up Time

A frozen river makes its way
down the rugged mountain side.

Melting into ribbons of streams,
some cascading waterfalls.

Glaciers receding rapidly—
Climate change reality.

(Alaska has about 100,000 glaciers, half the glaciers
of the world. In Alaska 616 glaciers are officially named. Exit
Glacier, not shown here, retreated 187 feet from 2013-2014,
from melting. It is estimated that if all the glaciers of the world
melted, sea level would rise over 200 feet, covering coastal cities.
There is no question that glaciers are melting. It is time to take
climate change seriously.)

Photos are Poems

Taking nature photographs,
    with rivers of glaciers flowing.

Silver, red, pink, chum, king salmon
    leaping waterfalls to spawn.

Brown bears grunting gratitude,
    growing fat for hibernation.

Tongue Licking Good

Black bear cubs of Alaska
  love to climb elderberry bushes.

Mother Nature's bountiful gifts,
  dripping with sweetness on the tongue.

Mother stands by protecting,
  mothers everywhere are awesome.

Pine grosbeaks, male and female,
  courting and cavorting air show.

Red males and yellow females,
  make a colorful sijo poem.

Mother Nature is the poet.
  I am a pen writing what I see.

Shining

I believe birds have a consciousness—
    This little nuthatch sat in my hand.

Looked deep into my eyes,
    before reaching down for a heart seed.

Wings are lifted up in gratitude—
    Light of infinity shining.

Healing

At the heart of nature
   is a deep feeling of beauty and wonder.

Heart Haiku captures this
   adventurous enlivenment.

Luring us toward meaningful lives,
   giving us new hope of healing.

(This book, Heart Sijo, is written as a companion of Heart Haiku. Seen together they show how one can easily move from one to the other in writing and teaching both formats of poetry.)

Gratitude

Today the fireweed is blazing,
    wearing its red blouses open.

Open for the bees to nuzzle,
    sweetness and nourishment for hive.

Baskets filled with sweetness—
    Grateful for the gift given.

A cascading waterfall,
     coming out of the misty clouds.

Giggling on its way to the sea,
     hurrying to get home again.

Red, silver, pink, chum, and king—
     Salmon waiting for doorbell to ring.

(This sijo captures the magic of salmon migration in Alaska. The young salmon, after hatching in streams, make their way to the ocean's womb where they grow to maturity. Then they make their way back to the stream in which they hatched. This journey is one of the wonders of nature. They spawn and die, becoming food for bears and other wildlife.) Salmon sustained the native Alaskans long before the canneries came and started shipping salmon to the world).

In Alaska salmon is king,
    bears hear the dinner bell ring.

Salmon swim in glacial melt,
    streams that no one owns.

I am happy seeking the gift,
    filling creel with nature's delight.

Salmon Pink Skies

Salmon is big in Alaska,
  even our skies are pink.

Pink, red, silver, chum, king,
  swim together in the same stream.

Navigating rapids and falls,
  greatest adventure of all.

You can leave your
iPhone at home.
Granddaddy has
built in gps and
fish locater.

The arctic char delicacy,
     gift of glacial melt streams.

Prize catch for dinner table,
     the fly fisherman's delight.

Nature's aim is to please.
     Happy is the one who receives.

D. Cole

D. Cole

Eagle Wish

Wild eagle glides like lightning bolt,
    strikes a raft of ducklings afloat.

One taken in taloned claws,
    snared by beauty, eyes glinting fire.

Wish to be a wild eagle—
    Emblazoned on stoles of saints.

Wise as an Owl

Grown crinkled as tan tree bark,
    dozing and waiting for the dark.

Whoo, whoo knew you were wise?
    Harry Potter, the wizard, knew.

Eyes speak secrets of heart sijo,
    secrets we can not see, but do!

(As a way to teach love for nature poetry,
I drew the Northern hawk owl and wrote the poem while
working with colored pencil drawings with my grandchildren
who loved the Harry Potter books.)

Sea gulls soar over the mountains.
Wing tips brushing the puffy clouds.
Lifting my spirit.

D. Cole

Heart Sijo

Over the snowy mountain,
    a sea gull is soaring.

Flapping wings writing a poem,
    using no alphabet words.

Inspired by blue skies, I will
    write my own Heart Sijo poems.

Our universe is full of
mysteries
too wonderful to understand.
Nothing more grand
than the union of two hearts
never to be apart!

D. Cole

My Heart Leaped

I saw this awesome cloud scene—
    Two hearts magically as one.

Memories trickle down my cheeks—
    Memories of parental love.

In the fields spring lilies blossom,
    opening star studded hands.

Antiquity

Dragonflies from antiquity,
    enjoying warm summer day.

A helicopter buzzing,
    landing on green lily pads.

Four wings flashing presence—
    The grebe just ate one!

Dwayne Cole

Tucked safely in Noah's ark,
    rocked in cradle of love.

Dragonflies buzzing around,
    painting rainbow colors.

Ready to seek the olive branch—
    Find peace in calm waters.

Mother Grebe opened her wings—
    Two baby grebes slide into water.

After hatching she carries them under wings
    for several weeks for protection.

If eyes are made for seeing,
    beauty needs no other reason for being.

Sweet Peace

Rounded the curve of hiking trail,
  saw field of fireweed dancing.

Swaying gently in the breeze—
  A kind of heavenly scene.

Gentle breeze, come fan my spirit,
  for my soul is fading.

(I use heaven in my poetry not as a place that has mansions and gold streets, but as a symbol of our heightened spiritual awareness. South Korean culture influenced by Confucianism has a similar view).

II.

In the solace of solitude,
    bees humming a lullaby.

I listened until my soul
    was filled with beauty and grace.

Pandemic fears are healed—
    Nature gives peace, sweet peace.

III.

Swaying in the gentle breeze—
    Fireweed glitters in my soul.

Feel the warmth of the rays,
    hold infinity in heart.

Wild and perfect for a season,
    perishing yet living forever!

IV.

Fireweed is strong and tenacious—
    The first to come back after a fire.

Deep roots protect from harm,
    tap into the goodness of nature.

I will tap into love of God—
    Grow a radiant faith.

Robed with Care

Sit among flowers, feel God's care.
Touch tassels of Jesus' robe.

Sit among flowers, care for children.
Touch Mother Theresa's robe.

Sit still, flowers teach kindness.
Touch Buddha's simple robe.

Eternity Blossoms

The world was created,
  one flower at a time.

Butterflies sipping nectar,
  bees singing the first love songs.

All nature comes alive—
  Humans join the chorus.

II.

Yellow sunlight, heaven's flower,
  come, sing our soul awake.

In your golden eye, sleeping
  loved ones come awake.

Flowers are blossoming—
  Eternity in our soul.

Mushroom Miracle

Rain and warm nights call them forth,
   like Lazarus from his grave.

Crowned with red and white
   polka-dotted flesh, they appear.

Mother protecting daughter,
   under umbrella of care.

Eden Blossoms

Worker bees sipping honey,
free as the gentle breeze.

In a Garden of Eden,
heaven's light shining on them.

What more sweetness could one ask,
than sipping nectar of the gods?

D. Cole

Garden Magic

When the world falls apart,
    keep a spring garden in your heart.

Flowers will still be giving,
    heart birds will still be singing.

Nature is a praise song—
    A symphony that makes us whole.

Celestial Poem

Star shaped flowers open,
     reaching for the heavens.

Each hiding the sun and moon,
     each a celestial poem.

God, the Poet of the world,
     whispers love and tender care.

The gentle summer breeze
sends a fragrant message.

I am desirable!
I am always available!

Passionate life force.
Fertility, flame, desire.

God cares for the flowers
and God cares for you.

Common Fireweed
Anchorage

D. Cole
5-25-13

Wildflowers

Tundra flowers sing for everyone,
a song of sweetness.

Mamma bear eats blueberries.
Cubs tumble in flowers.

God cares for the flowers—
Eden could be no finer.

(Colored pencil drawing I did with grandchildren while teaching poetry.)

D. Cole

"The moon is a friend for the lonesome to talk to."
—Carl Sandburg

Climbing Trees

Oh, Mighty Sitka spruce tree,
I want to climb to your top branches.

Poke the man in the moon
with my walking stick. No small trick!

I want to touch the robe of Luna—
I need to touch Infinity.

II.

The moon rises among the stars,
sits on top of Sitka spruce tree.

In the flower garden,
the night air is crisp and pleasant.

The moon shines for the lonely,
so they have someone to talk to.

(I did not go out in the yard and say, oh, the moon sits atop the
spruce tree—That would make a nice picture! Instead, for nights
and days I watched the moon making its arc across the sky. I
patiently waited for the right moment to capture the moon
kissing the uplifted lips of the spruce tree—That is photography
and poetry.)

I lie in bed and gaze at moon,
    Luna comes through window.

Caresses me with love—
    She does not like doors.

The moon prefers open windows,
    to touch and bless the soul.

Worm Moon Tree Buds

Passing the torch, the sinking sun
    kisses the rising moon.

The yawning earth blushes pink.
    Ground is thawing, worms wiggle.

The world is so very beautiful,
    my soul is bursting at the seams.

(Photo taken from our bedroom in Anchorage, Alaska, 3-27-2017).

Poet of the Universe
A Vision of Beauty and Goodness

Dwayne Cole

Moon-glow

Full moon is shining bright,
  caressing our naked skin.

Feeling the deep sensation
  in body and in spirit.

Becoming one with the mystery—
  Best wedding gift of all.

(Asian culture speaks of skin-ship. Marriage vows blossom into skin-ship!

Triangle Tree

Ole Mossy named his buddy—
    The Triangle Tree.

I wonder, do trees feel pride?
    Are they pleased with their uniqueness?

When I embrace the trees,
    I feel them pulling my heart strings.

Golden Coins

Birch trees dressed in golden gowns,
   admire image in mirror lake.

Open up the bank vaults,
   and store the golden images.

Sing with glee, frame for all to see—
   How blessed can we be?

(Photo taken at Cheney Lake in Anchorage.)

The Larch Conifer

Standing like a bronze statue,
weave a cloak fit for a king.

Birds with glowing feathers,
sing angelic songs of praise.

Rise up all creation!
Join in the angelic chorus.

(Larches grow to 148 feet tall, and are among the dominant
plants in the boreal forest of Alaska. Although they are conifers,
larches lose their needles in autumn.)

Trees Holding Hands

Trees stand together as one,
   holding hands and gazing in awe.

Chugach mountains writing
   orographic love notes to blue sky.

Be still and stand quietly, please—
   Art show is in progress.

D. Cole

54

Respect for Trees

Trees give us air we breathe.
    Saving our trees is essential.

Our future is foretold in trees.
    Hang tough through storms.

Show respect for all living things.
    Snowshoe hare hops across trail.

Nature Fix

Turpentine forest bathing,
    spruce tree sweetness fills the air.

Healing aromas fill my lungs,
    rousing my consciousness.

I become a spruce tree,
    shivers of energy enliven me.

(The Korean Forest Agency has attempted
to medicalize nature as a healing friend. Most major towns in
South Korea have access to a healing forest.
In South Korea, Buddhism blends naturally with the belief that
nature has a spirit,
the human body/soul are one with the soil. Alaska has an
abundance of evergreen trees,
plus large wildlife consisting of caribou, moose, and bear.)

Sunrise, spinning, spinning,
  a swirling dervish of beauty.

A fire dance of wonder—
  New Year's first Alpenglow sunrise.

Sky and earth become
  One, uniting all entities.

(Photo from my book, *Alpenglow Miracles: Fire Dance of Wonder*).

In the depth of winter I learned that there was within me an
invincible summer.—Albert Camus

I gazed into the snow storm,
    angel songs reverberating.

Dreaming what no mortal
    has dared to dream before.

Heaven is here, with us now.
    Smiling, I felt my loved ones.

I often walk snowy trails,
    hear Angel songs reverberating.

Dreaming what no mortal
    has dared to dream in the past.

Purity of heart is—
    How we treat others with tenderness.

Skiing a snowy trail,
    looking for beautiful things.

Between every two spruce trees,
    a new door opens to awe.

I felt waiting to be born—
    An Eternal spring season.

Snow has a language of its own—
    All that speech drifting down.

Each flake a word of purity,
    judging no one by color.

Covering all with beauty,
    inspiring all with—*Strength to Love*.

(This sijo is about social justice. The last line reveals this theme
of social justice by using, *Strength to Love*, one of Martin Luther
King, Jr.'s book titles. This book made a great contribution to
my ministry,)

Snow Sijo

Walking on a snowy trail,
    one feels enlivened.

Heaven is all around us,
    as well as over our heads.

Snow is from the pure land.
    Sent to cleanse our soul.

Sijo Humor

A little snowman decked in red,
    blue eyes and carrot nose.

Stood smiling in open arm pose—
    A nibble, nibble, crunch!

Bunny ate the carrot nose!
    Thank you, Mr. Snowman, for lunch.

(Photo taken at Whittier, Alaska)

Kittiwake

A small gull of Alaska,
    named for its "ki-ti-waak" call.

Seldom comes to land,
    but knows how to pick a home so grand.

Stand in awe, One with the magic—
    Feel pulse of universe!

Alpenglow Miracle

Morning comes for all living things—
    Oh to see the dazzling display.

To feel wonder in morning sky,
    a lover standing at the door.

Please come in a ribbon at a time.
    Shine in my life again and again.

(Photo and poem taken from my book,
Alpenglow Miracles: Fire Dance of Wonder)

Poetry is a Love Knot

Two dragonflies in love knot,
     hold on as they bang art page wings.

Settle on a flower stem sipping,
     quivering as one not wanting to part.

Tenderness freely given,
     tenderness willingly received.

Causing me to ponder,
     muse in deep thought.

How many kinds of love are there
     in our diverse universe?

Wisdom is receiving gift given—
     Celebrate tenderness!

Be Gentle With Nature's Beauty

Butterfly catcher,
    how many have you netted today?

Dancing in elfin garden,
    clasping hands in gleeful play.

Life is taking in beauty,
    gently releasing for others.

Garden Sijo

The world was created,
    one flower at a time.

Butterflies sipping nectar,
    bees singing the first love songs.

All nature comes alive—
    Humans join the chorus.

To see the world in a flower,
    Heaven in a butterfly.

Is to hold divinity in your hand—
    Eternity in your soul.

The One in many.
    The many in One.

Grandchild Bouquet

Flowers are only for a season,
    unless their name is grandchild.

Where do flowers end, grandchild begin—
    Both a bouquet of love.

Bright sunshine, flowers, grandchild's smile,
    what else could my soul desire?

Snowshoe silflaying in twilight,
    nibbling tender green leaves.

White snowshoe hind feet,
    soon dancing winter snow back in.

Nature's perfect camouflage,
    to hide from the hungry lynx.

Lynx

Beautiful lynx with golden eyes,
    merciless and treacherous eyes.

In a child's imagination,
    it was just a kitty cat.

Magic pulled out of a hat,
    descendant of the mythical Sphinx.

Garden Music

Music was invented
    in the Garden of Eden.

Flutter of butterfly and bees
    were first to sing joyful tune.

Go dancing in the garden—
    Find your joyful song again.

A red saddleback dragonfly,
    flapping four wings in bog.

Art book pages turning,
    bright blue eyes yearning.

As sky catches fire,
    my soul draws flame!

(Taken from my book, *Dragonfly Magic*).

Sandhill Crane Mating Dance

Sandhill crane dancing for mate,
    stretch wings, pump head, bow gracefully.

Nest to build, eggs on the way,
    nestlings to be raised.

Dance low, dance high, don't be too slow—
    Love waits for no one.

Mew Gull

Spring in the bog is really here!
    The Mew Gulls have returned.

Nothing short of amazing.
    Travel thousands of miles each year.

Life is so diverse,
    yet one in moving toward Beauty.

Birds are poems nature writes,
spreading songs of joy.

Bird eyes reveal wisdom,
from unknown secret realms.

Heart music of the soul,
an elixir of wonder.

Frank Green Photo

Waterlily Magic

Look at frog eyes, see stars sparkling,
night moon gleaming.

The whole universe is seen
in that lily pad magic.

Looking in dreamy orbs,
see universe with new meaning.

Good News

Prophet with raised nape,
 dressed in dark blue preacher's cape.

Piercing eyes that send a shudder,
 demons quake far and wide.

Beauty, wonder, and goodness
 overcome fear and doubt.

Fearless messenger from the sky,
   will perform for peanuts.

Small payment for lifting our spirit,
   on wings of inspiration.

Yes, Emily Dickinson,
   "Hope is the thing with feathers."

(Photos taken from my book, *WINGS OF INSPIRATION*:
Photos and Poems).

D. Cole

D. Cole

Snowshoe Hare

I love to play with bunnies—
    Mother Nature's awesome wonders.

Change color from white to brown,
    to match the color of the season.

Mother Nature protects her best,
    we have to do the rest.

Be Still and Know

Our postmodern age has been taught—
    It is a sin to waste time.

Nature shows the value of stillness.
    Learn from the snowshoe to sit.

Things get done the Tao way.
    A time and season for all things.

"I declare, this world is so beautiful that I can hardly believe it exists!"

—Ralph Waldo Emerson

When the news is so heartbreaking,
    I pray for the suffering and dying.

Go into nature for renewal,
    to be entertained by my friends.

Snowshoe bunny kicks up his heels,
    warmed by the sunlight.

Hide and Seek Game

Thousand-year-old Chinese painting,
    shows magpie harassing snowshoe.

German made Nikon camera,
    captures sport in Alaska.

Putting it in a Korean sijo—
    A culture expanding experience.

Snowshoes are nature's wonders—
   Evolution's calling card.

Color of fur molts seasonally,
   to match the color of the ground.

Expressing the desire to live,
   share beauty all around.

Autumn's Gifts

Birch leaves fluttering,
    autumn's beautiful gifts.

White-crowned sparrows freely fly,
    unconstrained by worldly weights.

Letting go of my burdens,
    I join the chorus of praise.

Dwayne Cole

Boreal Chickadee

Oh, wisdom of bird songs,
    what will you write for us today?

Come, awaken wonder with
    songs that flutter the heart.

What will you sing for today—
    Life is a precious gift.

Heart Sijo Hope

Chickadees have been seen
as symbols of good fortune.

With sparkling loving eyes,
bringing to all good luck wishes.

Hope is a songbird with good news
that perches in our soul.

D. Cole

Nature is not always kind!

Salmon spawning in nursery beds,
  busy doing parent work.

The eagle tips his white cap,
  in admiration of the labor of love.

Grabs a salmon in taloned claws,
  eaglets to be fed.

D. Cole

Swans

Two swans sail from azure sky,
   land barely leaving a ripple.

Float like a child's toy sail boats,
   full of spices from foreign shores.

Child stands in awe seeing,
   Santa delivering toys.

Sweet gifts from heaven come
   in tremors of sunlight.

Generous, tender, and luminous,
   gifts we cannot buy.

Heaven's glory comes down—
   Light we cannot see, yet eternally do.

Bronze Britches

November sun on the Chugachs,
    dresses the birch trees in bronze britches.

Each tree a tongue of fire,
    to sing songs of praise.

If eyes are made for seeing,
    beauty needs no other reason for being.

The Lone Leaf

As they grow older,
    leaves become more radiant.

Full of heaven's star light,
    in an often dark world, they shine.

This little light of mine,
    I am going to let it shine!

(Photo taken from my book, *Lone Leaf Dancing.*)

Sometimes the whole
world is a rainbow
drawing all into its
radiance.
Let it shine!
Let it shine!

D. Cole

Celestial Rainbows

Whole world is sometimes a rainbow,
    painted with angel wings.

I will paint for you a rainbow,
    and hang it in your soul.

Each new day will radiate
    gifts from the celestial realm!

"The light in Alaska in particular is so beautiful.
So beautiful! Such incredible light."—Sebastiao Salgado

In the wilds of Alaska,
the foothills of the Chugach.

A grandfather caring for family
found solace and tender love.

Alpenglow-ology was born—
Beauty, truth, goodness, and kindness.

"Climb the mountains and get their good tidings. Nature's peace
will flow into you as sunshine into trees." —John Muir

The mountains call me to climb them.
Be filled with their goodness.

On every peak there is a door,
opening to new revelations.

Divine peace flows freely to all—
Bringing the gift of hope.

Earth has no sorrow that earth can not heal. —John Muir

All of nature is endowed,
with transforming energy.

I am glad I live in a world,
where April flowers blossom.

The world comes alive in Spring,
as the songbirds knew it would.

Soul Awakening

When I contemplate in nature,
  I feel my soul ripening.

Opening to the beauty of God,
  the Poet of the world.

Bees and butterflies sing to me.
  Flowers blossom in the garden.

Oh, to live like a flower,
  brushing butterfly wings.

Wild and beautiful!
  Drenched in rain and bright sunshine.

Oh, to be a flower—
  In wildflowers angels sing!

Snow cricket friends ride lily boat,
   softly swaying in breeze.

Fall in nectar cup sweetness,
   sipping lily pad blessing.

Food of angels and elves,
   lily pad blessing divine.

All life is inter-related,
    inter connected as one.

You cannot cup a flower,
    without touching a star.

Stars in the sky live and die—
    There is star dust in our soul.

Flowers changed the world,
    one petal at a time.

To cup a flower in hand
    is to touch infinity.

Stars in the sky live and die—
    There is star dust in our soul.

A cold Arctic blast on mountains.
    Time to harvest gardens.

Little songbirds fluff feathers
    into a warm sleeping bag.

Draw light from an eternal realm.
    Heaven's light in our soul!

Family of Dall sheep grazing,
a common sight in Alaska.

Our beautiful animals—
The Last Frontier is truly wild.

Viewing re-wilds our lives.
Nurtures our animal soul.

Do you see what I see?
  Nature's pareidolia art.

Creation of Dall sheep from snow.
  Mother Nature's snow art.

Alaska's Dall sheep sleeping.
  Mountain climbing champions.

(Pareidolia is the tendency to perceive a specific image in a random or ambiguous visual pattern. Photo taken from our deck in Anchorage, Ak. Photo is unaltered.)

White Wedding Gown

In Anchorage, snow flakes are falling,
  whitening the whole landscape.

Clothing green Sitka spruce trees,
  in white flowing bridal gowns.

In snow gowns, Angels come calling,
  singing our soul awake.

Photos and Poems
by
DWAYNE COLE

Heart Sijo

Kindness is language known by all.
Kindness heals broken hearts.

Kindness heals the one giving it,
and the one receiving it.

Be kind in every step you take.
Snowshoe bunny sits on warm rock.

(I placed the rock where it catches warm sun rays for snowshoes
to sit on when temperatures drop. I don't know how to define
kindness, but this seems to be a step in right direction).

Sammy

As a child on the farm,
　I found a baby squirrel on ground.

Its parents did not come for it.
　I took Sammy home with me.

Fed him from medicine dropper.
　Squirrels grew dear to me.

(Sammy's Alaska cousins seem to know me).

Look what we found on Valentine Day—
    Two hearts touching as one!

Heart love holds in tenderness,
    healing hurt and bringing peace.

The ocean is the womb of life,
    giving many loving gifts.

Leaf Calligraphy

I like autumn best,
    with nature's colorful handwriting.

It is like spring time again—
    Every leaf is a flower.

Gently whispering to us—
    Heart poems of wondrous love.

In nature all is poetry—
    The sun coming up is a poem.

In sunrise, sky and earth become one.
    Poems write the world.

Change the poem. Change the world.
    Let the change begin with me.

On the mountain's highest peaks,
    the sun suddenly shines bright.

Poets of old climbed high mountains.
    See where earth ends, heaven begins.

Look, heaven's door opens wide—
    Life has new glowing pathway!

"And now these three remain: faith, hope and love. The greatest of these is love."

— I Corinthians 13:13

Faith is a songbird eating seeds,
from our open hands and heart.

Hope is all hearts beating as One,
fingertips tingling with **Love**.

Faith, Hope, Love—the essence of life,
soul taking wings and singing.

Cole Thomas Photo

Eyes of the Heart

My love, let me tell you—
    How I sing to keep the dark away.

In the moonlight the wolf howls,
    to show the pups the way.

When darkness descends all around,
    my soul leaps in joyful song!

COVID rages across the world,
    transforming our way of life.

Everything is in flux,
    in process of changing.

Seen with Heart Sijo poems,
    moon shines transforming everything.

Wolf Moon

Wolf Moon rises over Chugach,
    bringing magic to the night.

Shines on a lonely friend,
    invites to howl with the pack.

Success comes in running,
    hunting all night on the Chugach.

Flower Mind

When we view pansies,
    the world becomes a flower.

Our mothers are flowers,
    sharing kindness with us.

In Eden, we are all flowers—
    Remember to be kind.

How happy are the little redpolls,
    swirling around the seed dish.

Independent as stars,
    flashing the universe.

Tipping their red cap,
    to kindness and loving care.

The sky is awash with angels—
    Rosettes of energy.

Redpolls whiffling around seed dish,
    coming from an Audubon painting.

Jesus said, God cares for the birds,
    God cares for you and me.

The sky is awash with angels—
    Rosettes of energy.

Swaying beads of a rosary, clicking—
    faith, hope, and love.

Our lives lit with dawning light,
    letting the glory shine in.

Heaven's light, Shine on me,
    for I am fading.

When heavenly light shines—
    Soul takes wing and flies.

Kindness that is partial in us,
    is all-embracing in God.

One with Nature

As I write these sijo poems,
    I sit gazing at Chugach.

The mountains rise up before me,
    transformed by rainbow colored clouds.

Twelve years of mindful bonding,
    I am an Alpenglow sunrise.

On my deck I watch redpolls,
    falling like raspberry blossoms.

They whiffle and spin around,
    taking seeds from a dish,

Bears and moose often walk by—
    Nature rewilding my life.

Alpenglow Creativity

To look outward at Alpenglow
    is to look inward at our own shine.

Contemplating the outer world
    expands our inner world.

Oh the rapture of being still,
    being mysteriously alive!

Heaven's Glow

Trees and mountains become one,
    covered with purity blanket.

Snow clouds provide halo,
    adding eternity's glow.

Visions of heaven flowing,
    illumining my soul.

Dwayne Cole

Dwayne Cole

BEARS AND MOOSE OF ALASKA
Nature Poetry

Photos and Poems by Dwayne Cole

We often encounter bears and moose
   walking around our condo.

Wild nature keeps us alert,
   rewilding our lives with Wonder.

Rewilding gives new perspective on life—
   Our connectedness with nature.

Nature Conquers Fears

Met this moose on hiking trail.
    Seized by fear, I froze in tracks.

The moose looked at me,
    and continued to eat pushki blossoms.

Behind a tree, fears are conquered.
    How can I conquer other life fears?

Keep a child's spirit in your heart You will never grow old!
—Dwayne Cole

To enjoy the beauty of snowflakes,
it is necessary to build a snowman.

Cold fingers and toes,
button eyes and carrot nose.

How I long for childhood days,
when there were fewer tears.

Alpenglow Miracles:
Fire Dance of Wonder

Photos and Poems
by
Dwayne Cole

Only from the heart Can you touch the sky. —Rumi

It is only with the heart,
    that you can touch blue skies.

Unless you are the sunset,
    reaching pink fingers into the sky.

Dawn of Alpenglow Miracles:
    Fire Dance of Wonder.

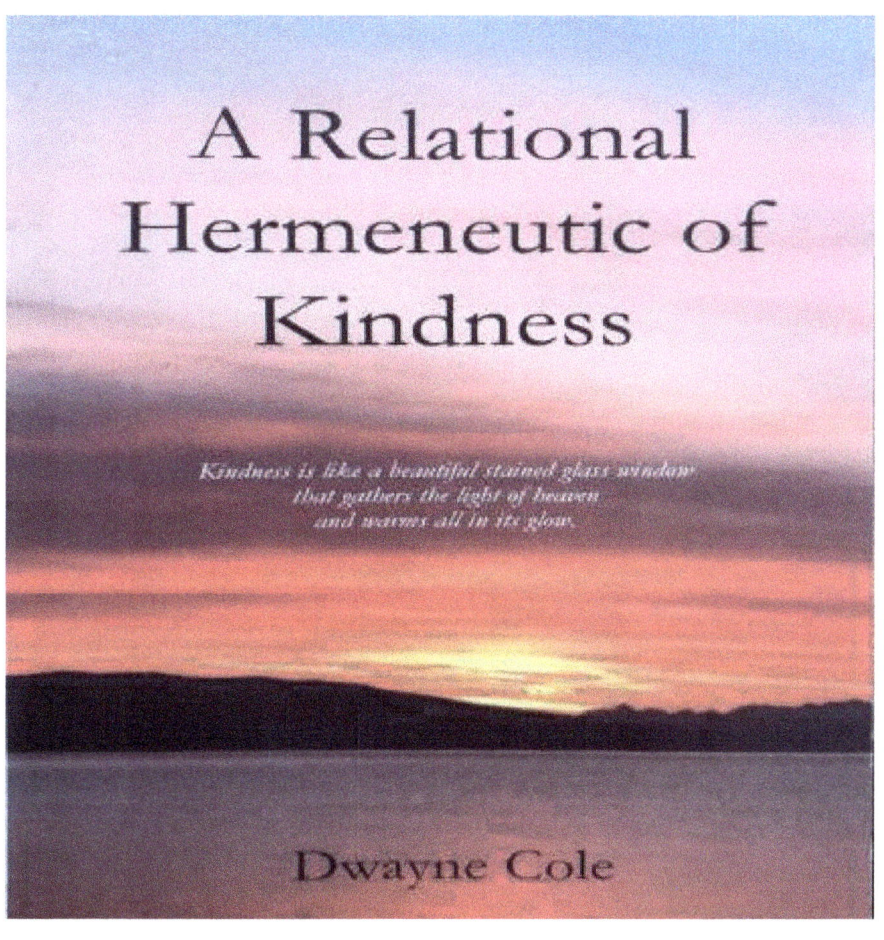

A Relational Hermeneutic of Kindness

Kindness is like a beautiful stained glass window
that gathers the light of heaven
and warms all in its glow.

Dwayne Cole

I believe in a world that is incomprehensibly beautiful
—an endless prospect of magic and wonder. —Ansel Adams

The light in Alaska
    is so very beautiful.

Relational kindness
    lights up the lover's heart.

Heart Sijo is a language
    known around the world.

Heart Sijo

Nature comes alive in me,
    when I write sijo poetry,

Forest bathing enlivens.
    Makes one more healthy and wise.

Joy comes in knowing we are one,
    with all other living things.

Conclusion

"In wildness is the preservation of the world." —Thoreau

Before humans existed
    they were a dream of God, the Poet.

Born from nature's wild things—
    Nurtured in the animal soul.

The wild enters into us,
    moving us toward Beauty.

To practice five things under all circumstances constitutes perfect virtue; these five are gravity, generosity of soul, sincerity, earnestness, and kindness.—Confucius

Faith in Unknown

As a Christian minister,
    I have sought to live a virtuous life.

A sincere earnest life of faith,
    marked by generosity and kindness.

And yet, our universe
    is marked by deep Mystery.

The biblical story of Genesis
    is a myth of how life began.

The "Big Bang" theory of science,
    may be real, or a myth also.

So I, will love the wild Beauty—
    The Wonder of being held in Love.

To say that something is a myth,
    does not mean it is untrue.

It means, it is more than true.
    Myth is clothed in Mystery.

I, will live Heart Sijo, until
    mystery becomes Reality.

OTHER BOOKS BY DWAYNE COLE

A Center that Holds: Adventures in Kindness

Alpenglow Miracles: Fire Dance of Wonder

A Prayer of Blessing: As You Go Remember This

A Relational Hermeneutic of Kindness

A Relational Trinity of Kindness

BEARS AND MOOSE OF ALASKA: Nature Poetry

Clouds of Inspiration

Down on the Farm in Georgia: A Poetic Memoir

Dragonfly Magic

Gentle Galilean Glories: The Tender Teachings of Jesus

God and Evil: An Ode to Kindness

Heart Haiku: Alaska Inspired Photos and Poems

Jesus' Transforming Beatitudes: Selected Sermons from Year A Jesus' Transforming Love: Selected Sermons from Year B

Jesus' Transforming Gentle Teachings: Selected Sermons from Year C

Kindness Is Every Step

Lone Leaf Dancing

Poems Inspired by Process Philosophy

Poet of the Universe: A Vision of Beauty and Goodness.

The Apostles' Creed: A Living Creed for the Living Church

The Bible: A Poetic Journey

The Book of Revelation: Jesus' Kindness Transforms Suffering

The Serenity Prayer: A Pathway to Peace and Happiness

The Story of the Bible: Authority, Inspiration, Canonization, and Translation

TREES AND DRIFTWOOD: Poetic Ecology

WINGS OF INSPIRATION

The next three pages are intentionally blank for space to write a few poems of your own.